Advance Praise for *Spooring*

The sharp energy of this poem, as it roams Italian mountains, calls us to our senses — as well as to sensory delight in a world of cicadas, juniper, barrelling clouds, the 'taste / of furzy space'. This is also a social, peopled landscape, full of signs, its many rhythms reflected in cuts and swerves through poetry, images and prose. Footnotes, inventively deployed as a parallel stream of attention, take the form of 'Roads grafted /onto other roads' that hook the route of the poem into the multiple universes of other texts, so that the impression is of travelling sideways, outwards and through one dimension and into others. It's in these traces of interlocking lives, and in the looping paths of understanding between them, that *Spooring* transforms images of rural locality, discovering the potential for new collectivities and encounters.

—Zoë Skoulding

In the interstices artfully assembled in Patrick Barron's *Spooring*, the "smack of the infinite" peeps out with evident appetite and curiosity. Although it appears to be a book, *Spooring* is less text than textile, interweaving lore, observations, terrestrial coordinates and bibliographic ruminants in a carefully layered fabric all its own, in the manner of riprap. An enthralling journey by a welcoming mind.

—Jed Rasula

Patrick Barron's *Spooring* is a radical act of attention. In sinuous poetry and lucid rushes of prose, he tracks the

Apennines in vivid granularity, pulling us forward to the next crumbling farmhouse, methane pipeline sign, or meal shared with a stranger. A polyphony of shelter and exposure, love and degradation, isolation and strange fellowship, his hybrid form is seduced by the berm and rooted the genius of the body, from "dust-caressed rocks" to insects who "spawn across the yawning/sidereal stone expanse." "Everything here/so precarious" he tells us, and yet with a "a little bit of sweat," we can learn to trace "a bliss that so playfully/painfully/ scampers off/again and/again."

—Karen Leona Anderson

Spooring makes a highly original and engaging contribution to the landscape of cartographic literature. As he walks and bikes down the Apennine chain, Patrick Barron combines personal narrative, lyrical poetry, maps, and photographs with the testimony of both earlier travelers and fellow writers in our own day. He even erects in his text many of the road-signs he comes upon, so that a reader too may encounter them.

Two things aspects of this rich chronicle of Barron's Italian journey were especially striking for me. One was the success of his multi-genre structure in evoking the pathos of so many Apennine hamlets--at once forlorn in their economic decline and depopulation and densely littered with the memories and other relics of their long histories. The other, the arresting images and stirring cadences of the author's own remarkable poetry.

—John Elder

Spooring

Patrick Barron

SPOORING
Copyright©2020 Patrick Barron
All Rights Reserved
Published by Unsolicited Press
Printed in the United States of America.
First Edition 2020.

All rights reserved. Printed in the United States of America. No part of this book may be used or reproduced in any manner whatsoever without written permission except in the case of brief quotations embodied in critical articles or reviews.

Attention schools and businesses: for discounted copies on large orders, please contact the publisher directly. Books are brought to the trade by Ingram.

For information contact:
Unsolicited Press
Portland, Oregon
www.unsolicitedpress.com
orders@unsolicitedpress.com
619-354-8005

Cover Design: Kathryn Gerhardt
Editor: Rebekah Stogner; S.R. Stewart
ISBN: 978-1-950730-33-9

Contents

I	7
II	42
III	95
Methodological Note	105
Illustrations	107
Translations of Signs	109
Footnote References	114

I

Passo della Futa. m. 903 slm. Now that the sound of my mother-in-law's car has faded, the intersection of alpine highways is silent save for the gusting wind and the hurried vehicle that intermittently passes, keeping me on edge as I walk into the dawn, wondering where the trail is. Not far from a burnt orange stuccoed roadhouse with forest green shutters and the look of missing patrons are two discolored metal plaques embedded in a grey stone wall, one commemorating the Mille Miglia, once a serious race now an antique car procession, and the other what seems to be a bicycle competition. Too much on the lookout for unsuspecting traffic and the lurking trail to read these indications of a slower era's races with care, even if they tend to humanize the road in grandiose whisperings at the margin, suggesting a time when travelers might have stopped to rest and take their bearings. As it is, I have trouble walking on the narrow shoulder. The wind is chilly and strong. It promises a fitful trip as it camouflages the sound of oncoming cars. There are striking contrasts between shade, sun, and limpid morning sky.[1] I step onto a triangle of scrubby plants and struggle with the map. Every pause has already become an exercise in reading it.

---

[1] The less the extent of atmosphere between the eye and the sphere of fire, the deeper is the blue colour, as may be seen even on low plains. Hence it follows, as I say, that the atmosphere assumes this azure hue by reason of the particles of moisture which catch the rays of the sun.

Walking
>that which wears
in the earth
>telltale stripes
that which wears
>us in
>>trailings of limbs
>pattering patterns
>spores
movements[2]
>>towards
>against
>steps inward
>>margins scratched
a lonely outside
>shadow
>curl of toe
>hackle of arches
>heels on the alert

---

[2] An analysis of the procession as a ritual might focus attention on its overall structure, the relation between authorizing texts and performance, and the deployment of decorative images and colors on carriages and flags to create auspicious outcomes.

            for that beyond
    that place
      within
        pacings'
       meditations'
    traces of feet[3]

Passo della Futa. m. 903 slm. The usual signs of a trailhead or widened shoulder appear, dirty plastic bags and crushed bottles, wads of toilet paper dropped on the ground. Ruts wind around a small rusty white building, a road construction storage container, a derelict transformer, a hunter's blind? Motorcycle tracks, invasive ivy, a downtrodden wood at the edge. My pace quickens as the wind yowls and abstruse clouds push through sun and shade in quick succession. I begin to hear voices and motors that don't exist.[4]

    It's not quantity
      but counting
    who could forget forgo
    let fall
      these worries

---

[3] I have loved the Mediterranean with a passion, no doubt because I am a northerner like so many others in whose footsteps I have followed.

[4] Sometimes, she dreams of an apparatus, an empty glass box that can be positioned in front of a window, into which a fragment of the world could likewise be positioned to ascertain the asymmetries in its patterns of causation.

                    loose as ankles
                        asleep
            or necklaces clinking
            into a bowl
                fingers pinching
                restricting the flow   PROPRIETÀ
                    links each a lapse   PRIVATA
                or a pause
                    a reason that laps
            against shores
                foreheads crossed
            with contagious notions
            deities or fantasies
                lacunae
                    woven
                        wormed through
                by numbers
                    obsessive numbers

Above Vucarelli. The shrill whirring arrives before a view of the metal mast, the sound of a sped-up cinematic sea, the roar of plastic waves. Slightly crooked, it rises 30 feet in the air in multiple sections, each joint arrayed with guide wires that run at steep angles to the earth. At its top a cross of sideways cups spins to measure the wind speed. Raspberries crawl along the edge of this brushy horizon, a disappearing clearing once a meadow perhaps a field cultivated with some sort of cereal.[5] They taste as they appear, a stinging pale red.[6] Through bushes a view of the mountains on either side of the Passo della Raticosa, 10 km or so to the north. Ferns, red clover, nettles tangle at my feet. Occasional shrubs and trees dot the grassy foreground. Each step, a tiny physical inkling that leads uphill.

CACCIA
DI CINGHIALI
CONSENTITA
SOLO A GRUPPI
CON PERMESSO

---

[5] Extant European barley landraces are largely confined to regions of rugged upland topography, such as the Alpine forelands and the Apennine spine of Italy. Landraces may no longer be present in certain areas because of environmental change or differing patterns of land use, or they were never collected in the first place from certain regions because of inaccessibility or political instabilities, etc. Moreover, inferring the respective contributions of different cultural episodes in the past to contemporary landrace biogeography is not a straightforward matter.

[6] What is this tint that in the shrill cress / Will never cease to trouble us and in the fields / Gives prick and praise for Beauty?

Derivations
>lines that lead
follow other lines
>nerves in nexuses
bursts rivulets gushings
of monotonies
punctuated ecstasies
then stases again
pushed downhill
through boulderfields of fates
into burrows
>beneath our feet
the urge more than an urge[7]
to express the excavation
vacancy vacillation
then plunging headfirst
along trails often
before thought
like this
>rendered minimally familiar[8]
then vanished behind heels

---

[7] A renewed desire to move among, "coursing," along, rather than at an oblique angle or distanced remove. To disregard the uncertainty of revision, the inadequacy of studied knowledge.

[8] Why should there have been such a dearth of poems on Italy? It could not be because men were not thinking of Italy, for they thought of few things so often. The question cannot be fully answered. But the fact remains that such poems were scarcely attempted until the beginning of the eighteenth century, and even then, with one or two exceptions, might about as well have been unwritten.

>   dust caressed rocks[9]
>   irregular yet ever faithful fickle
>   motions that orate gesticulate
>   life lives
>   patternings of feet
>   strides that hit
>   omit nothing

> *Mt. Gazzaro.* At the vague summit a rusty iron cross rises from a cinderblock alcove, nearly half a hut. Inside the alcove is a wormy altar with a thin sheet-metal box labeled in rough lettering "Libro di Mt. Gazzaro." Inside the box is a notebook with comments from visitors, some religious in nature, others appreciative of the air and view. A fragment of finely carved grey stone, perhaps a cross, lies in the dirt. Hunching down out of the wind I touch it with a finger.[10]

---

[9] Habitat: On the floor of clover and lucerne fields near orchards and sallows, willows and woodsheds. In attic beds and chairs next to communal webs. On ground covered in bramble, raspberry, rocks.

[10] And talking of the Alps and the Apennines, / The Pyrenean and the river Po, . . .

Musings-muzzlings
    a sniff of an idea
  lying in wait
      or hiding
  till the promise of sustenance
    materializes
      rooted fresh from earth's
    endless cellars
an idea
    frazzled, famished
in eternal gestation
      gesticulation
that bites its own heels
      in emergence
  or exiting
    last and first
in and of
    and without itself
a whiff of the extraordinary[11]

---

[11] Too often has vigorous growth appeared on this soil, in this air of Tuscany, for one to doubt cultural congeniality. Is there a repetitive afflatus here? Are certain techniques and attitudes with inherent affinities for each other so germane to a given physical situation that even after long desuetude resulting from

>   an extravagance
>   a whim
>   when uncovered
>   turned out
>   in turning to be
>   an inkling
>   speculative
>   indicative
>   of a cheerful
>   chary capsizing
>   a diligent
>   indigent digging
>   a wishing
>   wondrous
>   wishing[12]

00

Below il Poggiolino. Lying on a wooden bench near the stacked-up

---

war, economic collapse, or any number of other reasons, they will be "reborn" if the social ambience again becomes meet? Or is such repetitive flowering the product of deeply rooted, periodically dormant plants? Or is it a matter of coincidence?

[12] For the faith which sets the poet aglow we must go into the fields and hamlets of Italy, among the householders who were the descendants of the long line of Italian forefathers that had worshiped the same gods at the same altars—not gods of yesterday imported from Greece and Egypt and glittering with display, but the simple gods of farm and fold native to Italian soil.

remains of a hut, a few dishes spill out onto the ground, forks and spoons rusting among young nettles. A collapsible structure made of corrugated metal and fiberglass panels last used years ago. Where is its maker, its last user? Dead or too old for such a place? Traces of human activity tend to dominate my attention, however squalid. Beyond this shady alcove, many-colored flowers shudder in the wind.

    Whirls of wind
          howls however flower
  smattered
        gyres
            reelings
smack of the infinite
      yellow globes of swirling vortexes
   of pollen and petals
     grasses indissoluble
        from divine fronds
branches that breach the beyond
    clickings

>   chirpings
>   leaves sing
>   and ridges
>   remind
>   of the passage
>   taken
>   to come

Near ANTICO PASSO DELL'OSTERIA BRUCIATA 17 – 8 – 86. Oracular orange honeybee.[13] Green berries that emerge from drooping white flowers. How many thousands of people have walked through this seemingly solitary place? Hermits, heretics, monks, shepherds, healers, hunters, clairvoyants, misfits, gatherers? How much light-headedness, how much fatigue?[14]

>   Woodstock
>   of
>   fibers' fingers
>   grains of trunks
>   slim branches
>   growths
>   in rings

---

[13] She leaves the present defenseless in order to save the hereafter.

[14] The interaction between humans and mountains is poorly studied. The culture of mountain peoples, political geography of mountains, political ecology, and other areas dealing with the interaction between mountains and people are underrepresented in mountain literature.

scattered scratches
whorls that list to the side

Il Giogo. At the pass a fountain tap is open, the ground dry. I ask an old man with greasy hands stacking wood behind the only building, a closed restaurant, if there is a place where I can fill my bottle. Speaking partially in dialect, he brings me into the restaurant through a side door, then disappears down the hall. He reappears with a bottle of mineral water that is almost full and repeatedly assures me that "we used glasses." I thank him and walk across the deserted highway onto a dirt road under a sky that is now very cloudy.

DIVIETO DI SOSTA
LASCIATE LIBERO
IL PASSAGGIO

The animal pleasure of wandering
　abrupt spiny meadows
　　　scratchy trails
　　erasure of a fraction of the self
　　underfoot
　　miniexpansesexposures
　　　irradiations　　materializations
& then abysses in abundance[15]
　　　choked with green
　　that seem to ask
　　　　with what invisible

---

[15] Sky and earth, guard us from the monstrous abyss.

      impossible gumption
      in abeyance-subsidence
      abiding
      patiently waiting
           with shoulders to the wheel
   does this crawling-creeping earth
      keep at it?[16]

Poggio dei Prati Piani. A windblown orange tractor pulling a trailer filled with cut wood rolls up the steep dirt road with two old men atop, one with a white beard driving and the other almost bald standing on a rusty fender. Dust flies to the sides, and the gusts are so strong that the men have trouble staring at me.

---

[16] On the Adriatic slope below the 1000-meter level, there extends a hill country where Miocene and Pliocene clays and sands predominate. Here the wide valley floors of the consequent streams are filled with detritus, and the original valley walls have been badly gullied as a result of deforestation in ancient times. A poor type of cultivation, which has replaced the natural scrub vegetation, yields only scant returns, owing to the excessive sub-division of the landholdings. While this is particularly true of the Apennines of the Romagna, share farming (*mezzandria*) is widespread in the subalpine zone and on the Tuscan slope.

    Ridges worn out from looking so much[17]
       reaching so far
  into valleys sparse pockets
  of stubborn poverty
      here where the air seems clean
    water is hard to find
    and wild plants
       punish every move
  or wizen when winter
     whips up its flails
   ice wracks the sides of hills
or mountains that fluoresce
     flare aslant
   divers animals

---

[17] The transitional zone between Northern and Central Italy is somewhat ill-defined, but for convenience may be taken as stretching from the Cisa Pass to the headwaters of the Metauro River (Bocca Trabaria Pass); this coincides with what is normally marked on maps as the Etruscan Apennines. Folded Eocene rocks form the central mass of the range and three main rock types may be distinguished. Sandstones, known as *macingo*, provide the highest and outstanding relief features. Although frequently massive and often used as building stone, they contain much poorly cemented quartz and mica, and they are resistant only by comparison with the other rocks of the range. More extensive are the foliated and friable shales with which the macigno is imbedded. Their erodability and their tendency to become greasy and slippery have encouraged gullying and landslips on a vast scale. The third rock type, an impure marly limestone (*albarese*) is little better in this respect. Occasionally, where erosion has penetrated deeply enough, cretaceous limestone is exposed in which good building stones (*pietra forte*), much used in Florence, are quarried.

insects who await the chance
to spawn across the yawning
sidereal stone expanse

Capanna Marcone. Near dusk just uphill of the trail appears a stone hut with a stone roof whose door is open, the lock broken. Inside a table is littered with empty wine bottles and burnt-out votive candles. Rickety chairs are scattered around the room. The walls are full of black graffiti. Variously sized olive oil bottles sit on the mantle along with a small jar of salt and more votive candles. Plastic bags litter the floor, one partially wrapped around a carton of milk with a due date from last week. Outside it has started to rain and still the wind hasn't let up.[18] A truck passes by on the nearby dirt road in the direction of the highway, only a mile away. I consider spending the night here, but am worried who might arrive, expecting to find it empty. A group of teenagers with wine and sausages? A woodsman seeking shelter? I collect the trash and sweep the floor, saw and stack branches from a pile outside, then sit and listen with the door half open. I can barely read the map and try to envision myself sleeping here. The rain dies down, and as I walk out another two cars pass by. It unsettles me, and as I turn am surprised to see a small handwritten sign on

---

[18] Listen, listen, Mary mine, / To the whisper of the Apennine, / It bursts on the roof like the thunder's roar, / Or like the sea on a northern shore, / Heard in its raging ebb and flow / By the captives pent in the cave below.

a tree for a nearby mountain shelter.[19] I call the phone number, and a woman tells me that bed space is available. I eat a few raspberries and decide to forgo the hut for the certainty of human company.

      The vagaries of mapmaking
slopes that are flat
    fountains that appear out of nowhere
and a hovel that extends
    the empty invitation
      of the lines
    of a silent
        swarming trail[20]
first a thorny meadow
    then a rough road

---

[19] Where the arrows /   of the road signs /
    lead us

[20] The trail that runs along the Apennine ridgeline that divides Emilia Romagna and Tuscany carries the mysterious number of "00." In the fog or in dim light, the double zeros, painted over ubiquitous red and white stripes, appear as eyes looking backwards or off to the sides in the direction of real or imagined shortcuts or byways. These tangents, of which there are many, may prove overpowering to the woodland saunterer.

    that leads to a pass
        like the other passes
with only a slim shadow
of commerce
    ticks and traps
        unmarked
legions of leaves
    that point nowhere[21]
        a stone
    with fatigue
        that looks like thousands
of other stones
        shuddering boughs
      birds launched into flight
then a face
not a face
    a human
      crouched behind
            a knoll
      only
a knoll

Valdiccioli. The shelter is a recently renovated farmhouse complex hosting a children's summer camp. I seem to be the first outside guest of the season. The director, a tall man with the air of a priest, directs me to a spot on a bunk bed then explains how the wood-fired shower works and when and where dinner begins. He is trying to connect a computer up to the internet using his cell

---

[21] Geosphorical, graphical, a point in continual reticence.

phone, and I leave him to walk the grounds of the former farm. By now the sun has come out, but the children continue to play in the old stable. I feel a bit off guard, and despite having walked all day, am most at ease when I wander down an old dirt road and am out of sight of the house. I find a well, a small cave I am later told was used as a weapons cache by German troops during the Second World War, and former pastures that have been recently mown. Forested valleys and distant peaks undulate downhill to the south.[22] The drop-off at road's edge is steep, reminding me how high this place is. At dinner I am seated at one of the ends of the table and am flanked by rows of nine- and ten-year-old boys from Vinci, the birthplace of Leonardo da Vinci I am told with pride. The adults, who nearly outnumber the children, have colonized the other end of the table, and I am left to improvise conversation with a shy boy wearing a purple Fiorentina soccer jersey and an obese boy who within seconds of being served stains his face with chicken grease. Other children join in at intervals, curious about who I am and where I am from. After dinner I talk with the counselors, swapping anecdotes of former camps, and then retire to bed. I am already looking forward to the solitude of the morning path. As I fall asleep, a woman in the adjoining room begins to cough violently, a sound that mixes with the wind, now muted by the thick stone walls.

---

[22] In the mid-Holocene, palynological evidence suggests a distribution of *Picea excelsa* forests in the high montane belt of the Northern Apennines. These were subsequently replaced by mixed beech woods, including *Abies alba*. The climatic change of the late Holocene was the main factor that led *Picea excelsa* and *Abies alba* to become locally rare.

Sounds of fronds
in delicate balance
between gusts and soil[23]
    seeds interrupt
    flowers betray
             nurture
rupture
  feign indifference
    nettlesome roguish
    skies waffle
         intimidate
    scurry past
mountains bred from mountains
    madness
    & clarity
          in every false step
brusque movement
        stray creaking
             or hush
behind bushes
    the burrs of branches
        this tenacious tangle
of hair
of the meadow

---

[23] The exposure of catchment soils as forests became less dense may account for the increase in minerogenic in wash.

Poggio degli Allocchi. Circle-clusterings of beeches buffeted by wind with dense skirtings of leaves that seem walls.[24] Inside trunks sway slightly around a circle of cool shade. Outside swathes of meadow have been tilled up in muddy chunks by gangs of rooting boars.

A little tin hut
tucked in the woods[25]
crooked creature
of crooked creatures
you sport two stoves

---

[24] Rutilius, in the praise of Italy with which he begins book 2 of the *De reditu*, has a similar understanding of, in his case, landscape as fortification. The wisdom of god ("consilium dei") has erected the Apennines as a barrier, to serve as "watch posts over Latium" ("excubiis Latiis," 2.33); Rome is "encircled by multiple fortifications" ("multiplici ... munimine cingi," 2.39). In Rutilius' account a Stoic divine providence has organized the geography of Italy to provide the security for Rome that the Christians attributed to God and the martyrs.

[25] I long for shady cloisters where I might cheat death in illustrious style.

> two crooked chairs
> a warped table
> and an almost empty
> bottle of Vin Santo
> with you
> I toast the mountain
> so devoid of
> yet crowded
> with humans
> human remains

BESTIAME   ALLO STATO   BRADO[26]

Near Monte Giogo. Another hut, precariously sited on a narrow crest of friable earth. Inside dirty green fiberglass panels mute the sun making it seem that clouds have overcast the sky. I fiddle with remnants of occupation, scraps of paper, random empty salt and oil containers, a logbook with one illegible entry. On the floor lie woodchips, mouse turds, and a few cut branches ready for the stove. Squalid by

---

[26] The pastoral aspect of the economy of the Central Apennines has been much emphasized in modern literature, and sheep-keeping in this area has attracted most attention.

day, at night this place must be a wind-racked paradise.

METANODOTTO[27]

Passo del Muraglione. At the next pass a massive stone wall divides the highway down the middle. A snack at the deserted roadhouse filled with motorcycle memorabilia. There is a tired look in the eyes of the old man who serves me with slow aplomb. I recognize him from a walk I took that ended here ten years ago on the day of the second Palio in Siena, broadcast in the bar as I entered. This time, only one other customer arrives, eats a piadina, then rushes out into the windy dusk. A FOR SALE sign flutters as the door closes. I call M from an old telephone box, glad to hear her voice, then shoulder my pack. The old man seems to smile when I carry my plate and glass to the counter.

---

[27] Come quel fiume c'ha proprio cammino / prima dal Monte Viso 'nver' levante, / da la sinistra costa d'Apennino, // che si chiama Acquacheta suso, avante / che si divalli giù nel basso letto, / e a Forlì di quel nome è vacante, // rimbomba là sovra San Benedetto / de l'Alpe per cadere ad una scesa / ove dovea per mille esser recetto; // così, giù d'una ripa discoscesa, / trovammo risonar quell'acqua tinta, / sì che 'n poc' ora avria l'orecchia offesa.

VENDESI

Poggio di Giogo. An evening climb along an eastern slope of Monte Falterona.[28] Moments after the sun sets, I find a shallow fissure in the earth near the drop-off the trail has been skirting. Thin twisted beech trees reach up on either side of the opening, some dead, others alive.[29] I lay my tarp in the slightly concave bottom, making a blue cocoon, and then stretch out, checking for hidden stones and branches with my back. It seems someone hacked up the earth here with a giant cleaver. Perhaps it's a gun pit from the Second World War or the beginning of a slow landslide. Sitting up a last time, I look down into the darkening valley hundreds of feet below. I hope that the mountain stays put tonight, lean back and close my eyes, taking faith in the trees that are still alive.

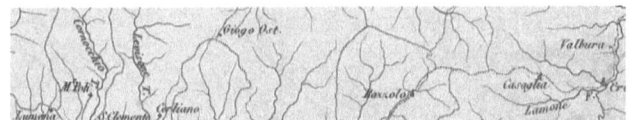

Mentions
    meditations

---

[28] The Falterona green black and silver: the formal sadness of the Falterona that swells up like an enormous petrified breaker, that leaves behind a cavalry of cracks and splits and chinks in the rock down to the sandy boiling up again of hills there on the Tuscan plain.

[29] The examination of a series of pollen records shows that *Fagus* appeared earlier in the western than the eastern part of the region during the mid-Holocene and became dominant in the northern Apennine forests post 3000 BP.

   a bit of pollen
         grasps it all
in loosening
      loses track
as seeds
       burst furrows
of other seeds
         in an orgy of seeds
         and seed casings
  fruit and fodder
 climb the walls
indicate
         the obfuscated
            obvious

tendril in hand
  a tiny tickling
communicant
with roots
      meters   upon   meters

              SODO
               DEI
             CONTI[30]

              Leaves
                      bloodstreams

---

[30] How happily you greet / the sun with your current, / in whose light you bubble to life, / ah, sacred spring, / daughter of the ancient forest.

        upwellings of faith
        forests that ask not[31]
        demand not that you
endure
    make a carnival
    of survival
        even if with so many
        artifacts in tow
    a continual orison
        with every breath
        and thought of you
        eyes dark and gleaming
        mysterious wells
shadowed
in hollows
            amorous
openings
    ready to speak
within
without
the sylvan floor

---

[31] These forests are the most important in the Apennines, if not in Italy. Straddling the border of Romagna and north-eastern Tuscany, they contain a huge variety of woodlands, some pure and some mixed, dominated by firs, beech and mountain ash, but richly interspersed with chestnut, elm, lime, yew and oak. Most of the woods have been untouched for centuries, and even now are only felled to meet the minimum requirements of good husbandry.

Passo della Calla. A stop at a small roadside bar to eat a sandwich. The owner, a man from Treviso with long grey hair wearing a red and black plaid lumberjack shirt and a brown wool hat, complains about a new tax law, the little money he makes, and the lack of appreciation people have for what he calls his "public service." He abruptly stands up and walks outside to smoke a cigarette.[32] I think of the old cheese, salami, and squashed bread weighing down my pack.

PURTROPPO
QUI
NON POSSO
ENTRARE

A few steps taken

and a universe

---

[32] From the economic point of view the area has little to recommend it. Cultivation has extended high into the mountains at the expense of the forests of oak, beech and chestnut, which survive in isolated patches and provide a meager livelihood for a few swineherds, foresters and charcoal burners. Grain and wines are the main crops grown, often on slopes which would seem to be best left undisturbed or re-afforested. As might be expected there is very little industry and over large areas population has been steadily drifting away to more favoured regions.

seems to have passed

a field of flowers

eddies within eddies

        flux that in stuttering
stalled
    for an instant

time to grasp
light[33]
    and its shadows

the making of an
expression

leaves' shudder

---

[33] The objects over there, traveling through the light, emerge from the void so as to have a place before our eyes. We are implicated in their appearing and disappearing, almost as if we were here for just that purpose. The external world needs those who observe and recount it, in order to exist.

a lone pebble
in a sea of stone

stubble
        an earth plucked
clean
        of pretense[34]

an appearance
        nearly
an appearance

Prato Bertone — Poggio Corniolo — Soci. Descent from the ridge[35] towards Soci, passing

---

[34] The Emilia Romagna slope of the Northern Apennines is strewn with over 32,000 landslides, 5,000 of which are larger than 1 million cubic metres. They represent the remains of geomorphic agents that shaped the Apennines during the Holocene.

[35] The geological structure of the Emilia-Romagnan and north Tuscan Apennines is characterised by intense folding with reverse faults, overthrusts and overturned anticlines. These features are a result of the orogenic movements which occurred

through the medieval monastery of Camaldoli, then a trail that leads under ancient chestnut trees along a decrepit stone aqueduct. Emerging from the woods, a wild boar startles me and I back up to the tall green metal gate of an old farmhouse. Inside a skinny man with one crooked eye chuckles and asks if I am afraid of boars. We start to chat about the mountain and soon an obese woman with long hair pulled back under a plaid scarf appears from behind a hedge and joins in. They moved here from Torino with their three daughters who I hear banging around in the kitchen. They seem starved for conversation, yet content to have the gate between us, locked with a bicycle chain. Continuing downhill, I encounter a series of chairs evenly spaced along the narrow trail. Minutes later while briefly walking the last few yards of a dirt road, I cross the meticulously groomed grounds of a modest farmhouse inn sporting a tiny wooden bridge and a cluster of gnome statuettes

---

during the upper Miocene. The region is still being uplifted and therefore continues to be affected by neotectonic activity.

near the road, then once again plunge into the woods. My suspicion that M and I once walked this way is confirmed by the familiar ruins of a stone house and a streambed crossing where we startled an antlered stag. Tired, I raise a hand to shield my eyes from the sun. It is almost 6pm and the wind has finally died down.[36]

TRANSITO VIETATO
AGLI AUTOVEICOLI

Gathered in
  at the corners
    pulled
      along the seams

---

[36] Under her eyelids closed / to the open sky Luni and the quavering / cities where the Apennines carry / a more human scent among sculpted / hedgerows amid the arable warmth of Tuscany, / or where they more wildly engulf / ancient churches in Etrurian earth

    ribbons
          streams
              ciliated
                seas'
apexes over apexes

xylophone-shores
                lap
                  lap
              at
        sand
      gravel
        rock

incrustations
of former seas'
    horizons'
      sewing[37]

  hands that rise
    in setting
            lines that mark
          the origin
      of beyond

---

[37] The analysis of shear wave polarization from a relatively large number of seismic events in [the] central Apennines has revealed a clear S-wave splitting. This feature affects at least the shallower portion of the crust (0–6 km).

a fossil future's
echelons

triangulations

echoes'
materializations

Soci.[38] Arrival at M's grandfather's house just in time for dinner. His caretaker, a Romanian woman who has lived in the village long enough to speak the local Italian fluently, tells me about her husband who works in Spain as we eat battered and fried sausages filled with cheese, a recipe from her hometown. That evening I walk with M's grandfather to the main piazza where a village festival is in full swing. Older couples are dancing to recorded music. Small children surround them and at intervals run screaming and laughing amidst the synchronized movements. We sit on folding chairs and watch the scene

---

[38] The hypotheses on the origins of the town are various: it is thought that there had already existed a Roman *castrum* or *vicus*, which was later abandoned due to plague or barbarian invasions; it is probable that a fortified village of feudal origin was founded around 1000AD by thousands of men, either free or under the protection of an area strongman.

along with scores of chatting pensioners. He has little to say, content it seems with gazing at this ritualized abandon. Back at home he runs a hand over his red 1947 Moto Guzzi motorcycle, then reverently pays homage to a browned newspaper clipping taped to the wall with a photo of Fausto Coppi, the early Italian bicycle champion, and one of Gino Bartali, Coppi's rival. He points out a dusty German helmet resting on a cabinet and briefly reminisces about the war. When he sighs deeply, letting his head drop, I know it is time for bed.

      Scents
            familiar scents
  nascent
      upcurlings
          wisps
          of cells

    bells ring in the hour
our comfort
the trap
    of waiting to be served
waiting for the end

flurries
  whispers become a buzz
    TV hiss our companion
not even newspapers'
ultimatums
gratings
heard in the continuum

                    the outpouring
            hold meaning
            any
            more

            meanwhile forgotten clothes
                        worn shoes
                            rags destined
                for some cryptic purpose
            the binding of wounds
            in our memories
                        hold
                the slight
            sad comfort
                that actions persist
            remain materialized
            in some faint form
                    if only partially
                    legible
            in their good intentions

                        FESTA DE L'UNITÀ[39]

Soci. I find my old mountain bike in the garage and decide to switch from walking to riding while still

---

[39] The festa system remains the only part of the traditional Church ritual schedule to have been firmly taken over by the Communists. It is significant to note that this is also the one aspect of the ritual system which is celebrated in public, outside of the cultic center.

attempting to follow the Apennine ridge.[40] I chart the beginning of an approximate route on trails and the smallest roads that I can locate on the maps at hand.

---

[40] Perceived wisdom suggests that its name [Apennine] derives from the Celtic "penn" which means "mountain," "summit," or "head" as in the headwaters of a river. "A-penn-inus" could have been applied to the mountain range by the time of the Celtic domination of northern Italy in the fourth century BC. [...] However, the name may not derive from Celtic at all but from Italic. When thinking of Italic, the mind automatically focuses on the heavily-documented dialect of Latium: Latin (with some of these speakers being involved in the founding of Rome). The problem with any idea of a Latin Italy is that there were in fact two distinct waves of Italic speakers who settled Italy, and these waves probably occurred hundreds of years apart.

II

PUNTO PANORAMICO

      Roads blossom
in grains
sands of slopes
  elopings of self
with space
   as landscapes
    rustle by
  perceptions
  caressings
  affections
    in every petal
   pedal
   push
to the limitless
mix
  panorama and mind
   that pant out partitions
     ensembles
  homages
  celebrations
       confessions
   rantings
some sort of rhyme

or hidden music[41]
plus
a careful
listless
listening

An elopement of minds'
surging sequences

past passes

---

[41] Each of us is happier following the flocks to pasture than anyone of you would be to go to a feast within your walls. We do not look for riches, nor other excitement than dances and songs and flowers and garlands.

    the wind speaks
           pearls of grains

    animal perception

        eyes in muzzles

    muses in the meadow

    tenses past the moment
in motion

    motes
the dust drama
    bones down the creek
enjambments of banks

      ankles
  inklings of antecedents

    who ceded
  the lineaments
    of soil
      this sacrament
      this parchment

            FONDO
            CHIUSO

Roads grafted
onto other roads[42]
thistled shoulders
worried woods
then thickets
and a hazy valley
that yawns
its evergreen self
to sleep
stalking paths
varied existences
my heart
yelps of hounds
breeze through the chestnuts
ferns and blackberries
perhaps an apricot
a glimmer of suns
between bands
of ultraviolet shade

---

[42] Directionless roads, all of them. At once I / stopped to think of it in just that way. / One might become stalled, thinking in too large / a containment and threaded every through and which way, / attracted to a loss. So huge, and yet not / uncommon complexity.

IMPIANTO CATTURA DIVIETO DI CACCIA

A bit of hazy midday
chatter
village posturing
near the pastures
flies
then leaves
and a mild trafficking
of tasks
gossip
would you
will I
ah that village
oh that village
hi
bye
glances stolen
taken for granted

CONFINE
DEL PARCO
RISPETTA
LA NATURA

Monte Faggiolo, near La Verna.[43] Pushing my bike through thick grass and nettles along an abandoned road at dusk, I find a metal hut with a rusty oil barrel stove. The 1997 newspapers inside a clear sign of disuse. I gather wood, start a fire and cover a hole in the top of the stove with a white rock. Not long after, as the wood crackles and flames reach the top of the stove, there is a loud explosion. The stone has blown apart, spraying small white fragments everywhere. Shaken but unharmed, I melt cheese on bread and stretch out on the wooden floor to eat, gazing out at the dim pines. Smoke is leaking

---

[43] Is it rash to hazard the suggestion that Dante's description of the Earthly Paradise was based on the life at the monastery of La Verna in the Casentino? It was here that S. Francis received the Stigmata. At this monastery S. Bonaventura wrote, in 1259, the *Intinerarium Mentis in Deum*. Dante knew the neighbourhood well (*Infer.* 29^{109}, 30^{65}, 30^{73}, *Purg.*. 5^{94}, 14^{43}, *Canzone* XI, *Ep.*, ii, tit.). It was perched high up by the crest of a spur of the Apennines. Here the air was clear and cool, and in the forest close at hand the sweet breeze moved whisperingly through the tremulous leaves. Here the birds, the little sisters dear to S. Francis, sang joyous and undisturbed. Here hyacinth, anemone and narcissus carpeted the ground. This Franciscan retreat was indeed the summit of a mountain climbed by penitence, discipline and love. Here man's pristine innocence was restored and his happiness regained.

out of myriad rust holes, but as long as I stay close to the floor I can breathe.

SENTIERO 50

Meadows
within you
meadows
around you
light touches
intense
brushings
against
twinned
fates
feet along
the same path
hands coupled
rocking
with the wind
minds
inside
flowers
outside
the slopes
elope with us
mild surprises
around
each bend
or twist

>of affection
>tendrils
>curling
>together

SENTIERO 50

Monte Faggiolo. The nettles despite their nastiness are quite stunning in the sunlight, shuddering in the breeze around things passed out of memory.

>A mountaintop
>   prairie
>   whose seeds
>   breezes
>   vistas and rolling
>   space
>   emit delights
> prickly waves
> of flowers and grass
> acres of grace
> bounded by arbors
> secret sylvan eruptions
> splintering ravines

>   thunderheads
>   thrust past
>   by a wild wind
>   whorls of endless
>   patience
>   placeless
>   speed

Near Pieve Santo Stefano. Emerging from the woods on a steep winding road in light rain, I coast to the valley floor then pass under Superstrada E45.[44] Paralleling it, I slowly ride along a quiet byway. Later the byway again crosses the highway, this time passing over it, and to the right from out of a concrete slab so weed-strewn it seems a meadow rises an old stone monument to the Virgin Mary, returned it seems near its original position after the highway was built in the 1970s. Plastic flowers glimmer in the sunlight that has just emerged as large trucks thunder by somewhere underneath.

O PASSEGGERO
CHE PASSA PER VIA
NON TI SCORDAR
DI SALUTAR MARIA

——— • ———

GIOVACCHINO BONACCI
ERESSE L'ANNO 1902

---

[44] Visiting motorists ... ought to be warned to drive defensively on that 60-mile highway across the sullen ranges of the Apennines; during peak periods an alternative route may be preferable.

ATTENTI
AL TUBO

        Frames
        of pieces
        particulate matter
          switchbacks
          and fountains
          the run of rays
          sun-bleached signs
        lines along the road
        reduced to blotches
          specks
          next to
          miles upon miles
        of stonework[45]
        sly
        meadows
        bushy woods

---

[45] About thirty yards within the gateway rose a square tower, lofty enough to be a very prominent object in the landscape, and more than sufficiently massive in proportion to its height. Its antiquity was evidently such that, in a climate of more abundant moisture, the ivy would have mantled it from head to foot in a garment that might, by this time, have been centuries old, though ever new. In the dry Italian air, however, Nature had only so far adopted this old pile of stonework as to cover almost every hand's-breadth of it with close-clinging lichens and yellow moss; and the immemorial growth of these kindly productions rendered the general hue of the tower soft and venerable, and took away the aspect of nakedness which would have made its age drearier than now.

　　　　　　　　　winkings at my back

　　　　　　　　　　　DIVIETO
　　　　　　　　　　　　DI
　　　　　　　　　　　SCARICO

　　　　　　　　　　Clouds barrel past
　　　　　　　　　　forests speak in
　　　　　　　　　　tongues
　　　　　　　　　　flowers tipsy with wind
　　　　　　　　　　cast glances petals
　　　　　　　　　　my way
PERICOLO　　　　　　your way
DI INCENDIO　　　　 with
　　　　　　　　　　water
　　　　　　　　　　that trickles
　　　　　　　　　　into the basin
　　　　　　　　　　into the ditch
　　　　　　　　　　with its mawful of
　　　　　　　　　　weeds
　　　　　　　　　　rootlets of trees

AZIENDA
FAUNISTICO
VENATORIA
SINTIGLIANO

Near Cerbaiolo. A farmer tinkers with a tractor as a dog gazes through swaying grasses at trees and clouds.

CACCIA CONSENTITA
AI SOLI AUTORIZZATI

Near Montelabreve. I stare at the map, trying to make sense of how to proceed, to avoid wrong turns. A few insects crawl over my skin, itchy already after a chilly night wrapped in most of my clothes and a thin sleeping bag. Every so often a firefly passed in front of my closed eyes, startling me with its lightening-like glow. At some point I was awoken by a loud animal crying out in what seemed a cross between a bleating sheep, a howling dog, and a honking goose, all being stabbed.[46] The animal moved quickly to various parts of the valley below, then came close to where I was stretched out on the ground. When I turned my flashlight on and shouted, it kept its distance.

S. ANTONIO[47]

---

[46] these fangs of ours / are perfect / for this ice . / what flung the ice is also near

[47] He is a gigantic figure who, if standing, would tower far above his tormentors. He has been meditating on the Crucifix on his knees and has been occupied in reading the Holy Writ. But now, he glances pathetically upwards and spreads out his

1935

The contentedness
  of a late morning swim
chilly mountain waters
  swirl in a dark hole
embracing the myriad
  invisible organisms
and darkness and cold
  plunging in
head awash
  with upstream particulates
and an overwhelming
  sense of health[48]
the timeless crush of waters
  all in their place
the sense that so many
  relatives human
nonhuman kin
  have swum
and dried themselves

---

hands in a gesture of lamentation as he receives a ferocious beating from a small greenish devil.

[48] We have begun to realize that we are indeed living in the mountains, and that spirit of the Apennines enters into our hearts day by day. There is a peculiar joyousness in the light pure air that raises our spirits to a perfect exhilaration; we feel inclined to go into raptures over everything, and take all human creatures around us into our overflowing affections.

in sunny meadows
perfumed with youth

DIVIETO DI PESCA
ZONA DI PROTEZIONE

Parchiule. A long descent through the Alpi della Luna on a winding gravel road. At the bottom of the gorge a small abandoned village comes into sight on a high ridge, its yellowish walls giving out on a grey outcrop.[49] Later a group of old woodcutters hack at tree trunks and branches pulled from uphill slopes. At Parchiule there rises next to the gravel road a large dome-shaped mound of vertically stacked branches on a circular area of blackened flattened earth. A single light bulb hangs above the center of the mound, and a small wooden hut sits off to the side. A wrinkled man who walks out of the woods with ashy hands tells me that that they still need to "put the earth on." Then it can be lit "from the top, not the bottom."

---

[49] There's nobody living anymore / in the pink house in front of the field / where they used to have the horse fair. / The shutters creak and are falling apart piece by piece / and inside there's a peach-tree growing / from a pit that somebody threw away.

FRANA !

Mercatello sul Metáuro. It begins to rain and I stop for lunch at the Taverna del Cacciatore, a restaurant in a postwar yellow concrete building at the edge of town. At the table next to mine sits an itinerant hardware salesman who orders a steak. The restaurant owner declares that the water we are drinking comes from the highest commercial spring in the Alps, then later wonders aloud why "we Italians are so fixated with drinking water from other places." When I leave the rain has stopped and the road glistens.

>   Vespers
>   vigils
>   of kempt
>   fields
>   unkempt
>   woods
>   hushed whispers
>   preindustrial fibers
>   filigrees of stuff
>   we were once
>   made of
>   then again
>   harpsichord serenades
>   cicadas
>   serendipitous
>   thunderings
>   storms in the distance
>   cloudycoolweather

        and gusts always
         gusts
of what
the hills or skies
provide
    it is thus
that systems and fidelities
the vast realm of spirits
  living and dead
  are knitted together
in a weave
    always frayed
fraying
  of splotchy vision
    sun and shade
inside the eye

CADUTI MASSI

Near San Martino del Piano.
In the lee
  under the protection
of an ancient

       lichened oak
as orange as green as yellow
    as black as grey
   then a stray dog
as yellow as brown
   stops to scratch itself
      salute-inspect myself
sunrays
        under the empty windows
       of an old farmhouse
   that leans out
with one shade half-drawn
   pulled to the side
the rest
        all missing but one
half
     an eye
keeping watch
   on the roses
hazelnuts
       mulberries
and nearly empty
    courtyard-driveway
with raindrops
    and gravel
      witness to so many
tasks
    then silence
   silent passings
       of passersby

Near Piàn della Sera. In a glance at the end of a long uphill climb it's clear that the place is abandoned, shutters open or missing, a dark spot in the roof that must mean a hole.[50] An hour before sunset, dogs are barking from nearby farms, a bird squawks nearby. Briars[51] and nettles grow thick along and in the path. Before long this passage will be all thorns. At the top of the hill the threshold comes into view. Steps covered by dust and loose local stones. A 1986 agricultural magazine with photographs of sheep and combines lies rumpled next to a rusty oil company bucket containing mechanical parts. Above a broken window, thin white wires are tacked in place to wood beams infested with burrowing insects. I hear their rasping and think of my own house made of wood. Down a short hallway is the wreckage of broken timbers, roofing tiles, moldy plaster and reeds. The combination kitchen and dining room's

AZIENDA
FAUNISTICO
VENATORIA

---

[50] Like marginal environments everywhere, say the desert edge or the moist tropical forest, the Mediterranean mountains have a finite carrying capacity, a maximum threshold population, which changes with levels of technology and productivity. But they also have a minimum threshold, a population level beneath which labor shortage presents agriculture in all but the garden spots. Mountain agriculture needs many hands and backs, because few labor-saving devices apply, and terraces and irrigation ditches require constant surveillance and maintenance.

[51] Shh! hack le raw jaw claw / Briar author 1/2 notes: / (perfect patch blew / Byrds nommo / Stuck in your / Que? Que? Que? / "Bomba, Plena, Salsa, Rain dance / War dance, Magical Invective...

lone fireplace is full of broken wine bottles. Other rooms are still intact but show cracks in their thick stone walls. One contains a pile of white rags and a box of unopened soda bottles. Another, the slender white ribs of a small animal. I don't feel safe investigating the central chambers and wander in and out of peripheral doorways. Stalls with abundant rotting hay, a chapel whose blue collapsing ceiling reveals a blue evening sky, storage rooms with demijohns and a plow. More rooms out of reach, sight.[52] Too many brambles or too much risk. Beams everywhere sag, flooring tiles, hanging askew, threaten to drop. The narrow hallway leading from the front door seems the most stable place. I sweep away debris and dust with some of the white rags and lay my blue tarp down. Soon the setting sun fills the threshold with coppery light that warms the auburn stone.[53]

On the threshold
of an unstable
    farmhouse cluster
  stables chapel
      living quarters
  for who knows

---

[52] The architectural structure of a building is not exclusively the result of technical and aesthetic influences, but depends also on a combination of other factors: from those most closely linked to the physical environment, such as geology, morphology, and climate, to economic, historical and anthropological conditions.

[53] Mild and clear is the night and without wind, and quietly above the roofs and among the orchards the moon rests and reveals clear in the distance every mountain.

                how many
    ants creep
    spiders await
        timbers sag or are already broken
    with their weight
        of rot water and woodworms
                        whose steady
        consuming song
                mixes with
            crickets
                    a distant band
        the odd car
            and a baying-barking
                    now and again

Near Piàn della Sera. At dawn I hear a car pull up, then men and dogs in the brush. Probably hunters in training. I assume they have no interest in where I am and continue half-asleep to hear them. About an hour later they leave, and then so do I.

MONUMENTO ISOLATO[54]

Below
  ridges
    lap ridges[55]
    ringed
    cut through
   by valleys
    a horizon
     at every angle
    of the head
  spin of the eyes[56]
there's
  a motion
   a rolling
    into
   out
   of place
  from shrine
  to shrine
   Antonio

---

[54] The mountainous nature of the Apennine is indicated both by the colossal dimensions of the statue and by the stalactites which cover it. The water falls from the mouth of the monster, whose head the god presses, into a great pool below.

[55] At the regional scale, steep slopes had the highest species diversity, the greatest exclusive species richness and a steep rarefaction curve. The diversity pattern of cryophilous taxa was not related to the general pattern of total species richness, with these species being more common in three habitat types with extreme environmental conditions: ridges, cliffs, and screes.

[56] The mountain is wheeling around, and my brain has gone for a spin.

    Maria
     Rita
      the saints
       keep watch
      peer
     from behind bushes
     outcroppings
    make sure
   we stop
  slow our thoughts
remember
 for an instant
  the purity-impurity
   of leaves' speech
 wings'
measurement
 meditation
  of mountaintop
  to mountaintop[57]
trailing the debris
 of moments
  movements
   over the land
    hearts throbbing

---

[57] In the sun's eye I sate, nor deemed his ray / Too bright to gaze on for the autumnal breeze, / Though gently whispering thro' the yet green trees, / Was cool and humid, and around me lay, / Toss'd like the billows of some mighty bay, / Etruria's Apennines, range over range, / Swelling in long and wave like-interchange

> full throttle
>   then nearly stopped
>   at the stupor
>   beatitude
>   of an altitude
>   sparks aflutter
>   heels alit

DISCARICO
IN SEQUESTRO
GIUDIZIARIO

Between Piàn della Sera and Pietralunga. Miles upon miles of rolling road, steep hillcrests one after the other, nearly no road signs. It's well before noon and it seems that I've already climbed two mountain passes. Not sure where I am in this arid brushland of sparse farms, all that I can do is continue south into the increasing heat.

CASA PERICOLANTE

> Everything here
> so precarious
> in arrears
> jerrybuilt

if left alone
crumbles almost
at once
bones of bones
reused
or forgotten
in fields
that accumulate[58]
grasses upon
grasses
then slide
frayed
dirt
and stone
towards
an eventual
inevitable
sea

ANTICHITÀ

Above Pietralunga. A garage that from a distance seemed a bar contains a woman skinning two chickens. Minutes before, a man let me fill up my bottle from a tap affixed to a cowshed. He kindly insisted that I let the water run

---

[58] For instance, ancient patterns of settlement have by now vanished into the ground; but life continues over those same sites within a substantially similar, or at least recognizable, physical framework, even though today's pattern of living may be not of long standing.

until it was cool. The morning's series of climbs is over and all I can see is a distant, wide valley that extends for miles to the south toward Gubbio. I can just make out the long descent ahead, winding in and out of oak woodlands.[59] Elated, caressed by a gentle wind, I gaze out over the land.

Nearly embarked
on a fresh start
not so
nearly weary
tires burning up
the road[60]
the road burning
us up
supplications
supplications
we bow

---

[59] Monarch of the woodland is the Oak, of all trees most dear to us who live in northern lands. It is celebrated in literature from the earliest times, indeed, of no tree has more been written than of the Oak.

[60] how / much would be chucked if this versus / then forest of Arden / should burn in the name of the national hamlet

to the debris
the detritus
of passage
perception
the waking
of sound
of all that
scattered
across the morasses
abandoned niches
obvious
occult cracks[61]
serpentine
fissures
in this hard
hard ground

PERCORSO PITTORESCO

Near Poggio Parrano. I finally escape from the heat and traffic of the Via Flaminia and exit

---

[61] The latter, on the other hand, definitely *are* tombs. They are often very badly preserved, but it is clear that the original form of the monuments was a small cairn covering a slab-built cist, which was sometimes preceded by a short dry stone passage. The bottom is frequently paved.

into Gubbio. After a leisurely lunch and walk in the center, I slowly make my way up a narrow gravel road towards the Passo del Termine.[62] A man appears from behind a shed and cautions, "It's so hot. Try not to exaggerate." Every so often I lie down on crushed limestone in the shade of a bush or tree and try to regain a small measure of energy.[63]

"the runoff from the mountain
was collected for defensive purposes"

"only after many vicissitudes"[64]

"an almost pollution-free countryside"

"together with breathtaking panoramic views"

---

[62] The scenery was wild and stern in the extreme, the hills, like most of the Apennines, bare of trees and consequently scoured by every little watercourse down to the bare rock of gravelly moraine. At the foot of this ascent, which takes the road to 2300 or 2400 feet above the sea, we pulled up according to custom at a cottage, whence a pair of oxen with yoke and ropes were attached to the pole in front of our poor weary jades.

[63] But who sows lime over the Apennines? This fluffing of the sense is often apparent in the rendering of prepositions.

[64] On the 5th of June, 1349, a servant, whom Petrarch had sent to inquire about some alarming accounts of the travelers that had gone abroad, returned sooner than he was expected, and showed by his face that he brought no pleasant tidings. Petrarch was writing—the pen fell from his hand. "What news do you bring?" "Very bad news! Your two friends, in crossing the Apennines, were attacked by robbers."

Passo del Termine—Molinaccio Umbro—Fiuminata. A descent through a valley nearly lost in time, fortified hilltop villages, woods, and farms. The only cars I see in two hours, approaching from opposite directions, meet exactly at the point where I have stopped to gaze over a precipitous drop-off, one foot resting on the guardrail.[65] They are forced to slow down, and I laugh to myself at the absurd intersection of paths. That night I sleep in Fiuminata in the town's only hotel in a room with a balcony overlooking a garden. I treat myself to dinner at the restaurant downstairs, a generous serving of fettuccine with truffles. Just before midnight there is a brief bonfire of cardboard boxes that lights up an acre of village.

CURIOSITÀ
NATURALE

---

[65] We are what the seas / have made us / / longingly immense / / the very veery / on the fence

A warehouse
or cemetery
it's hard to tell
from up here
among the bales of hay
drifts of wind
grass stalks clattering
against themselves myself[66]
at the scruffy margin
looking out upon
a world of scythed plants
the drool of a city
mountains out of reach
temperatures steadily rising
I feel a fever over
everything
the pine bark is sweating
ants
if things keep on like this

---

[66] little lapping sounds   yes / as of dry grass secretly drinking   try again

dry heaves will come[67]
reminding me
of how human
and animal
and fragile
this organism is

Eyes betray
so much
  curiosity
curling
coddling
  of lips
a wisp
of a glance
  oceans of
pupils
irradiating
dilating irises
  they take in
what they're
able

---

[67] Nothing outside can cure you but everything's outside.

    told
      don't want
    to see
    the slow
    movements
     of hands
    over hands
    bodies
      massings
    separations
    of bodies
      tides of flesh
    urbanized
    yet
    outgrowths
     of a pungent
    earth
    that even
    when
    seemingly
    silent
     is a writhing
    tangle
    of beings
    eating
      beings[68]

---

[68] Then, before the very eyes of Simplicius, Baldanders changes into a scribe who writes these lines [...] and then into a mighty oak, a sow, a sausage, a piece of excrement, a field of clover, a white flower, a mulberry tree, and a silk carpet.

Today / still too tired / for much utterance / much thought / in this heat / not so bad considering / what it could be like / torrential downpours / locust storms / infestations of ticks / and yet something / inside me / is wilting / waiting for evening / and some release / a chance to move / then rest / in a small patch / of woods / somewhere along the gravelly-grassy road[69] / a little higher up / a bit of sweat / some slight peace / of mind

                Covered by cicadas[70]
                          and serpentine
          arbors
                the wood worms its way
        into song
                    and flight
        overhead
              within the head
            room for sight

---

[69] down . . . gentle slope . . . boreen . . . giant aspens . . . wind in the boughs . . . faint sea . . .

[70] stumble into spaces between / the expanding and contracting / membrane song of the cicada

scattered apertures
           operations of blue
that move in synch
   with quavering
      chlorophyll arrowheads
a dawning
   and a darkening
in bark
   as in clay
            clouds of junipers
      arrays of vines
the slender explosions
of trunks in unison
            in supplications
offerings
of exchange
   of delay

                              IN CASO
                              DI NEVE
                              O GELO

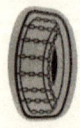

I lie here
smothered in my own
mutterings

monologues of heat[71]
scattershot cicadas
incessant pesterings of flies
as the sun seems
affixed in its sky
as if the night of recovery
uneven sleep
unfamiliar sounds
will never come
or come too soon
and the accusation hangs
in the torrid air
that this time on my hands
this ride across Italy
may be
an exuberance
a flagrant skulking
worth at most
a poem or two[72]

---

[71] too tardy to listen to the locals / too obligatory to pray, unmediated / too much of an image to scurry / too turtle to be hedgehog-ish

[72] In the three centuries from 1500 to 1800, notwithstanding the notable interest in Italy as evidenced in a great variety of ways, the number of English poems written in that period that have Italy as their theme can be numbered on the fingers. The dramatists, it is true, often lay the scenes of their plays in Italy, because in many cases the stories they borrow are Italian, and they are almost inevitably compelled now and then to depict an Italian scene. But the poets in general either ignore Italy altogether or touch on it only incidentally in passing. As we

>   and little else
>   Hurrah!

Near Torre Beregna. Another tangle of roadside forest nearly 1000 meters above the sea, a mild cacophony of stationary farm animals and random insects, wild beasts.

> The Sybillini
>   shards
>   of a former
>   future world
>   winking in
>   the day
> so far above
> the roosters
> valley traffic
>   early
>   baying dog
>   yet utterly
>   aligned
> and aligning
> with these few
> small tasks
> of morning
>   ablution
>   opening
>   perception

---

approached our own time, however, we find the poems on Italy increasingly in number until they cannot be enumerated in detail in a paper a brief as the present one.

rising

VENDESI
CASA IN MONTAGNA[73]

      A hyperreal edge
      of the dawn[74]
      yet tangible
      as the smoky air
      tinge of sweat
      bells ringing
      in the hour

---

[73] In lands of old civilization and dense settlement the progressive depopulation of mountainous areas, with the abandonment of fields and dwellings, is a well known phenomenon.

[74] O star of morning and of liberty! / O bringer of the light, whose splendor shines / Above the darkness of the Apennines, / Forerunner of the day that is to be! / The voices of the city and the sea, / The voices of the mountains and the pines, / Repeat thy song, till the familiar lines / Are footpaths for the thought of Italy!

>—6:45—
>a peasant-priestly
>precision
>so civil
>so entrenched
>nearly
>untouchable
>by clocks
>now in phones
>(I check mine
>to be sure)
>one hand
>in the present
>and one
>in another
>in this present
>prescient reality
>give me an abyss
>give me a kiss
>I could almost
>launch myself
>over the edge[75]

A stone unearthed
a bit of earth tilled
for seedlings
of thought

---

[75] But the only way to elude the human landscape that is striking us would be to walk faster into the air, to fly.... There: I, too, feel suspended as if over a precipice....

a worming
wearing in
of intentions
good
intentions
one
on top
of another

PUNTO TURISTICO

Amandola. Sitting in the shade at a bar under a portico. A teenage girl appears with a "Viva Las Vegas My Kind of Town" tee-shirt.[76] She loiters next to a stone column for a while with a confused look then wanders off. A sun-bleached foreign couple cross the square, pensioners go about their rounds, a teenage boy shows off his new sunglasses and clothes, groups of women recently emerged from church congregate and chat. At this bar are families with children, a primped woman in white with a small black dog, an old man with a cane, a few cyclists. At the other bar a few meters away is a gaggle of old men with beer and cards. Through the square an incessant procession flows by of

---

[76] Architects have been bewitched by a single element of the Italian landscape: the piazza. Its traditional, pedestrian-scale, and intricately enclosed space is easier to handle than the spatial sprawl of Route 66 and Los Angeles. Architects have been brought up on Space, and enclosed space is the easiest to handle.

motorcycles, three-wheeled Apecars, bicycles, cars, and pedestrians. A curious girl in a flowery dress prances about with a box of juice. A large group of churchgoers suddenly appears, dominating attention with their animated talk. An Apecar with an elderly couple heads out of town, the woman wistfully gazing at the mob. Bells begin to ring. Sparrows soar by. More well-dressed people arrive and the gab gets thicker, louder. A bare-chested obese man with long hair and a cigarette in his mouth leans out of a window at the top floor of a brick building overlooking the square. His expression is blank.

    An avenue of selves
    each in its variable
    moveable niche
motions toward
around one another
jokes behind cupped hands
a singling out
gazing every so often
out the window
    to long
    grow accustomed
    give in and join hands
    let certain questions
    take root or rot
cast out
within
behind the mind.

Grottamare—San Pietro Avellana. All day riding towards the coast in torrid weather, I arrive on the beach in Grottamare just before sunset, dump bike on the sand, kick off boots and socks, then dive into the azure water.[77] I spend the next day with friends and their children among crowds of other young families and pensioners. A long series of stalls selling clothing and seaside toys, people eating ice cream, hundreds of baby strollers in an unending procession under the lee of palm trees, aging villas, and large modern hotels. I sleep on a cot next to the stove and listen at night to the sounds of a fussing baby. In the morning a small train inland to San Pietro Avellana then pedaling towards Capracotta.

Weeds come together / till brush becomes / woods becomes forest / that bequeaths itself / over / and again[78]

---

[77] Far from the Pirin, the pointy Apennines plummet toward the sea.

[78] "A place for wild nature, surrounded by mountains and full of woods," said Francesco dei Vieri of the Medici villa of Pratolino in 1586. Della Bella found it the same in 1653, when he made a series of large prints of the villa and its grounds.

Near Capracotta. In search of empty houses with roofs still intact, perhaps a window or two and minimal trash, a respite from country so open that distance breaks a person open, forcing a reconsideration why what really matters is so far away. Each step at this juncture a little more, a little less.

DIVIETO DI:
CACCIA-PESCA
PASCOLO-TRANSITO

Currents
        upwellings of fronds
slender willow leaves
    sabers that waver
               whisper
in their tiny multitudinous
        colonies of faded
    flushed
ferns near the bottom
    of the abyss
    lower still
    giant leaved hearts

Terminating the north axis from the villa was a great basin and a gigantic statue representing the Apennine mountains. The statue still exists, though the grotto behind it has tumbled down, and no modern visitor mentions the rooms inside the colossus painted to show men mining precious ores.

> then oaks roses locusts olives[79]
>   all in chaotic
>   arrays-waves
> with a sinking-sucking in
> of the lower gut
>   an effect
>   of high places
> and
>   a depth of field
> impossible to enter
>   render asunder[80]
>   with descriptions
>   only tentative
> explorations
>   sinkings
>   of eye ear
>   skin nose and mouth
>   the time it takes

---

[79] We know that gentians grow on the Alps, and olives on the Apennines; but we do not enough conceive for ourselves that variegated mosaic of the world's surface which a bird sees in its migration, that difference between the district of the gentian and of the olive which the stork and the swallow see far off, as they lean upon the sirocco wind.

[80] Chi puo contar l'esercito chemosso / Questo di contra Carlo ha 'l re Agramante, / Contera ancora in su l'ombroso dosso / Del silvoso Apennin tutte le piante; / Dira quante onde, quando e ilmar piu grosso, / Bagnano i piedi al Mauritano Atlante

> a gust to carry
>   a certain flavor
> of a leaf
>   from stem
>   to tongue
> a calculation
>   a taste
>   of furzy space
> distance
>   measured by
>   affective
>   perception
> reception
>   of particles
> lenticels
>   of
>   motes
> cuticle ticklings
>   fingertips
>   barely
>   touched

DIVIETO DI:
ACCESSO, RACCOLTA DI FUNGHI
TARTUFI, E PRODOTTI DEL BOSCO

Vastogirardi. Fireflies as far as the eye can see along this pitch-black road to the trail to the woods where I am camped.⁸¹ Before I turn off, a voice coming from the opposite direction calls out, "Who's there?" I respond, "One who enjoys an evening stroll." We exchange the standard greeting and pass, two masked shapes with momentary voices. Not far away is an ancient Samnite temple and a clear mountain spring.⁸²

    A stretch
      of solitary
     bustling woods
      traffic at my back
   a ditch by my feet
    an abundance of stone
   the occasional leaf
   yellowed
     by summer frost
 or sun
     some extreme
   typical of the place
   and the pummeling

---

⁸¹ In the early 1960s, owing to air and water pollution in the countryside (our blue rivers and limpid irrigation ditches), fireflies began to disappear. The phenomenon was rapid and terrible. After a few years the fireflies were gone.

⁸² The mediaeval church of Sant'Angelo was built on the remains of the holy building. Sant'Angelo inherited his pastoral vocation from the ancient pagan divinity, often superimposing his cult. The Italic temple, surrounded by a portico and protected by a polygonal masonry enclosure, stands on a tall podium, with central steps, 4-column pronaos at the front and a single cella.

        the seasons dish out
     meanwhile the dimness
      between spindly trunks
         must hide
       myriad invisible eyes
     that catch my presence
         move on
      around or through
        the few rays
        to illuminate
           green-grey bark

DAL BALCONE
DI QUESTA CASA
DAL 1911, VIENE
RAPPRESENTATO
IL VOLO
DELL'ANGELO

———

ADDI' I LUGLIO 2001
L'AMMINISTRAZIONE
COMMUNALE

Near Pietrabbondante.

    Mowing over the remains
        of an ancient world[83]
   the world looks on
   and over
        stones
    monuments to strife
 fatigue
     festivities
        and mourning
or simply not simply farming
the shepherding
        of sheep cattle goats
and the incidental passing of time
   steps taken
      in wandering
  from cunei over cuniculi[84]

ALLEVAMENTO
SELVAGGINA

       Bushels of clouds
       grains of rains
       falling in the distance

---

[83] Livy characterised the Samnite people as *montani atque agrestes* [...] and Salmon's study reaffirms the tradition of a rustic backwater thinly populated, especially by shepherds and herdsmen.

[84] To Aesernian [Hercul]les, [-?- Or]fius, for favour granted, gave (this) as a gift to the grove

    here a creaking of insects
    muted roar of traffic
    thudding of wheels
    on a tiny bridge
    here flowers as tall as houses
    a tree twenty times
    the size of the village
    perched on an upwelling of rock[85]

    QUI NON SI FA CREDITO

    flakes of forest shattered by lightening
        dawn's arrows of needles and twigs catch fire

STRADA PRATICABILE
CON DIFFICOLTÀ

Campobasso. A long, exhausting day across Molise to a former village sprawled into a random city. Farmyards squeezed between highways and illegal buildings, chickens prowling near the center in a place that seems an outskirt, tenements that look as if they're ready to

---

[85] the longest song edges back in & makes its demands on the nature of the apparition

collapse.[86] To find a hotel requires riding to the far side of town beyond a military police barracks and into an area that with its vacant lots, small factories, gas stations, chain stores, fields, and piles of trash could be almost anyplace. I soon see a sign that proclaims in bold yellow letters "HOTEL EDEN." In front a few men in tailored suits walk across a spacious lawn of worn-out Astroturf.[87] From the narrow windows of my top floor room is a view down on a farm shanty surrounded by piles of scrap metal, more bands of roaming chickens, and a family in greasy clothes gathered under a sheet metal overhang. Just beyond is a vast junkyard, and in the far distance the mountains from where I came.

In a city with few tourists
an outsider seems quite the rarity
no great curiosity
perhaps incredulity
as the funeral spectators await

---

[86] In topographical terms, much of the Mezzogiorno in the 1980s resembled a building site. With increasing affluence and the return of many migrants from abroad, a wave of wildcat building swept through the South.

[87] The grass sprightly as Astroturf / in the September frost / and a mist / here where the ground is low

on benches in this little piazza
two pensioners and myself
a young girl and her younger sister
the usual-unusual assortment of passersby
through this rather sprawling and ugly city
with monuments of little importance
to the vast outpouring of Italy
but nothing to sneeze at
for an American
as children play and shout
as the funeral reaches its finale
the hearse's trap door is open[88]
the spectacle of mourning
is about to begin
only six or so in attendance
one screams at a young boy
the end is something of an anticlimax
perhaps someone ill for years
in any event
a ceremony performed
seemingly out of duty
with little obvious mourning

Campobasso. The fuzzy TV has a bad western in this diner with the air of a truck stop out of some '50s American film like *Bus Stop*, the owner's kids playing cards, traffic outside and the slick of rain off wheels. A Padre Pio calendar, a no smoking sign, wood paneling

---

[88] Hark, you that sigh! / Life is a pin-point / Stuck in death's sky, / Holding the firmament up

with gold stripes, a military police certificate of thanks. Something comforting here, yet also threatened and threatening. It brings to mind a childhood trip with my mother and sister back across the US from Connecticut to Montana, divorce proceedings already a foregone conclusion, our car on the verge of breaking down. Here the traffic is incessant, and many signs point to people barely getting by. I'm the only client, like so many other nights. Across the highway is a new shopping center, swamped with cars.

VIETATO
FUMARE

Reflections
wheels
selves
gatherings passings
leaves hit the ground
acres of grout
stones at their limit
a barking
at the edge of home
glottises loosen
throats in operation
a shout
a fragment of shell

cigarette butts and a piece
of broken plant
never again
will the piazza
be quite like this   STRADA
                        SDRUCCIOLEVOLE

        An underpass
          offering
               to meadows above
     how to slip past
           sylvan growth
    or shine with it
      dive below
   hoping not to offend
      watery
             spirits
   ripples
      at the limits
   of our eyes[89]

---

[89] YE Apennines! with all your fertile vales / Deeply embosomed, and your winding shores / Of either sea—an Islander by birth, / A Mountaineer by habit, would resound / Your praise, in meet accordance with your claims / Bestowed by Nature, or from man's great deeds / Inherited:— presumptuous thought!—it fled / Like vapour, like a towering cloud, dissolved.

    Were you were I to extend
        a splayed tentacle
across the divide
    what might
            ignite
  bind
      take root in our minds
    hearts all aflutter
      selves dissolved
            made
suprareal[90]
a numbness come
            to
               glitter?

---

[90] When it is borne in mind that Ovid was born in one of the most picturesque tracts of the whole of Italy—the rugged highlands of the Abruzzi, not far from the highest peak of the Apennines, the huge Gran Sasso d'Italia, with its snowy covering that lasts throughout most of the year—it might have been expected that the landscapes of his native district would have evoked his enthusiasm, or would, at least, have found appreciative reference in his poetry.

      Words crossed with sticks
        with kinks
          and crooked inklings
of matter
    with thorns
        lairs of wrinkles
at the ends of alleys
    tiny thought
      enclaves
        peekings out
from leaves' interstices
    bushes' coughings
        the instance of a slip
    light loosened in a glimmer
some slight sign
      of affirmation
exposition
    of our inner operation

        ZONA MILITARE
        INVALICABILE[91]

---

[91] Tier upon tier it towered, the terrible Apennines: No sanctuary there for wings, not flares nor landing-lines.

III

Napoli. In the morning a train to Napoli and a musician friend living in the upper Spanish Quarter. I ride from the station through swarming scooters, cars, and pedestrians, then carry my bike to the fourth floor of an old apartment building. The door is open, and I find my friend with his landlord and a drummer from Tunisia on a terrace that overlooks the bay and the island of Capri. We squeeze giant lemons into glasses of lukewarm tap water and enjoy the view. That evening we walk through the neighborhood, chatting with acquaintances who regularly appear from out of the crowd. Mutts of all sizes weave their way through cars and pedestrians. Dinner with a skinny Ukrainian photographer who keeps taking pictures of the cooks, a free concert of Calabrian pop-rock, a walking tour of street graffiti until past midnight. I drag myself out of bed at 6 am and ride back to the station through a city already full of traffic to catch a train south to Agropoli.

DIVIETO ASSOLUTO
DI SCARICO

>   Once in a while
>   an upwelling of orange
>   mountains drowned
>   in their own slumber[92]

---

[92] But Addison, in the year 1700, "proceeded in his journey to Italy, which," says Dr Johnson, "he surveyed with the eyes of a poet"; and from Geneva he addressed his poetical *Letter from Italy* (1701) to Lord Halifax, in which, among other subjects

an incision of city
bright as a lamprey
citizens snoring in unison
a single dwelling
cut of such cloth
what chance does it have
what mark will it make?

A last gasp
of solitary wandering[93]
watching others
as I write
wrestle
wrangle
seek

---

then new to English poetry, we find the mention of hills and mountains, the scenery of which, evidently from his own words, he seems to have enjoyed. Cf.: "How am I pleased to search the hills and woods" (I. 17); and it is here in this poem, probably for the first time in the century, that a poet of the age of Pope is found to speak of hills and mountains in terms of approbation.

[93] Walking at three kilometers an hour, we begin to perceive and to understand the problems of the mountains.

to finesse
a feeling of layered
perceptions
condensations
a touch of angles
investigated all at once
or steeples
and crypts
embraced
held at arm's length
considered
mulled over
nearly *ad nauseum*
yet nerves
of
gazes
eyes on the alert
intercede
interrupt
corrupt
keep clean
my senses
sense of intersections[94]

---

[94] And this familiarity with geographical conditions will be of help even when we come to deal with such ethereal things as the works of the poets—in the case of Italy, where there is so much in the outer world to affect sensitive natures, one is tempted to say that it will then be especially of help.

ROVINE
PERICOLO DI CROLLO

Between Ascea and Pisciotta. The road along the coast is lined with trash from start to finish, bottles, bags, diapers, tires. The sea is an azure field hundreds of feet below. The temperature steadily rises as I climb and descend, staying as close to the shoulder as possible to avoid the steady traffic. Not long after lunchtime I take a sharp turn and see on the opposite side of a gorge a steep grade of new asphalt with a flashing red light. Before this new test I lie down on the lip of a drop-off under a row of planted pines, taking care to avoid scorpions that may be hidden in the needle litter. The flashing light indicates a section of repeatedly repaved road that is being carried towards the sea in a slow landslide. A car not downshifting in time stalls then struggles to restart.

NO BORSE

Whence arrived
the cracking open
bursting forward
bustling to concretize
to make some sense
of momentary
fossilizations
years after their dissolutions
there also appeared
a pressing
in moving
in place
to elaborate
bring to the table
a reappropriation
of process

Between Palinuro and Marina di Camerota. I arrive at the shore exhausted and sweaty and push my bike through the pine trees and sand[95] to where last year I came with old friends I know must be somewhere close by. I find them at a small makeshift café under umbrellas eating ice cream. Happy to be once again with people who know me, we chat for a while, then all dive into the sea. Relieved to be at last immersed in the sea that all day

---

[95] In the same manner as in several parts of the Apennines, where the ground is light and loose, I have heard the same kind of sound on stamping with the foot.

glimmered below the highway cliffs, I look forward to the days in good company ahead.

DIVIETO DI TRANSITO

An arbor
of disconcerted
    harmonies
layer after layer
longings after sky
        azure infinitudes
    spyings through stems
        leaves' laughter
            impersonal
            calming
    prickles the air
my eyes
that narrow
    open
    seek shade
silent pathways
    meridian interstices
  some poor
  protecting
  camouflage

RIFUGIO NON ACCESSIBILE

Marina di Camerota—Camerota—Monte Croce di Calvario. Days spent at a slow pace, each morning a swim at dawn off sharp rocks in clear waters under the lee of an ancient tower, afternoons at the beach, trading time in the water, the pinewoods, the makeshift café. My friends introduce me to S, a teacher and farmer, who leads us on an all-day hike through the countryside across abandoned fields and brushy woodland. He enthusiastically reveals traces of former worlds, bringing us into the folds of Monte Croce di Calvario.[96] We drink from wells hidden under rocks, visit olive groves, eat small plums in thickets, dig up and chew licorice root, breathe the vapors of incense trees, and lunch on goat ricotta, tomatoes, jam, and bread. The day ends with a descent through intense afternoon heat to the beach. We

---

[96] Proceeding to the west, over the plain which extends between the two summits, another object arrests still more the attention of the observer. The summits themselves have no crater, nor any vestiges of one; but these vestiges are sufficiently evident on the sides of the plain; which here sinks into a cavity, which may be about three hundred feet in length, from east to west, above two hundred in breadth, and one hundred and sixty in depth.

peel off sweaty clothes and jump into the water, gazing every so often up at the dry slopes just descended.

In the shade
    of an idea
        germinal
        with carapaces in place
    yet swollen
           with promise
              whispers
a tendency to exceed
        exude daydreams' residue
    of a bliss
        that so playfully
           painfully
  scampers off
        again and
           again

VIETATO ATTRAVERSARE I BINARI

Piciotta-Palinuro—Naples—Rome—Arezzo—Soci—Bologna. Feverish for the last few days in Marina di Camerota, hard to keep my spirits up. Departure by train at dawn and arrival in Rome[97] by late afternoon, where feeling worse, I fall asleep in the sweltering station while waiting for my connection, which I miss.[98] The farthest I can make it is Arezzo, where there is a citywide celebration underway called "Le Notti Bianchi." The next day I reach Soci, convalesce, then make my way back to Bologna, where threading through the center carries me back to the house where the journey started.

---

[97] Looking out from Rome due eastward, beyond the nearer heights that bound the Campagna, vague shapes rise in the blue of the distance, cloudlike, part of the atmosphere that encircles the City that is a world, or, if the day so decree, clear and defined, like frontier sentinels on the watch. These masses and peaks are the rough edges of a wall that shuts in a land, strange, uncouth, primitive, little distant from Rome in mileage, incalculably distant in everything else.

[98] Passengers take down their luggage, lift their bodies through the forest.

Methodological Note

In first attempting to write this book—a retracing of a journey on foot, then by bike, down the Apennine Mountains in central and southern Italy—I wasn't feeling my way so much as thinking it. And the process should, at least in some measure, be the other way around. I went back to the beginning and revisited my notebooks, reconsidering the sensations of making my way along paths not nearly as untrammeled and forgotten as they pretend to be. The result is a collection of indications, invocations, interpretations, interactions, signpostings. The genre is mixed. Poems trade places with short prose passages and transcriptions of road signs left in the original Italian, translations of which appear in endnotes at the end. Footnotes interrupt throughout, tempting fragments and byways. There are also a few photographs and maps.

The project is inspired in part by Robert Smithson's idea that "language should find itself in the physical world, and not end up locked in an idea in somebody's head," and also the corollary—that the physical world can find itself in language.[1] Any text risks fossilizing ideas, and perhaps all the more so texts that take as their inspiration the physical world, since the overpowering immediacy of certain places tends to trick us into believing that language generated in response or dialogue will remain somehow authentic to those places. And the heady state of the cross-country walker is vulnerable to corruption, to believing that an empathetic dialectic with the physical world is translatable. To connect ideas to matter, thoughts to place, through language engaged with language. Not a fixed relief map, but a moveable index of small traces, tracks, words, and images, messages half-dismantled, enough to begin a paragraph or stanza, but not necessarily to finish.

---

[1] Smithson, Robert. "Cultural Confinement." *Robert Smithson: The Collected Writings.* Edited by Jack Flam. Berkeley: The University of California Press, 1996.

Illustrations

The six map details in the book are from the following sources, listed below in the order that they appear (all photographs are my own):

1-2. Details showing "Futa Dog." and "Giogo Ost." are from: Inghirami, Giovanni. *Carta geometrica della Toscana.* [1829]. Map. https://brbl-dl.library.yale.edu/vufind/Record/4167361

3. Detail showing "Falterona" and "Casentino" is from: Lafréry, Antoine, Paolo Forlani, and Giacomo Gastaldi. *Geografia tavole moderne di Geografia.* [1575?]. Map. https://www.loc.gov/resource/g3200m.gct00087/

4. Detail showing "Fiuminata" is from: *Umbria overo Ducato di Spoleto.* [1640-1643]. Map. https://orbis.library.yale.edu/vwebv/holdingsInfo?bibId=12793706

5. Detail showing "Nocera," "Dentecane," and "Campobasso," is from: Mercator, Gerard. *Abruzzo et Terra di Lavoro / per Gerardum Mercatorem.* [1613-1619] Map. https://brbl-dl.library.yale.edu/vufind/Record/4219909?image_id=15824668

6. Detail showing "Pisciotta," "Camerota" and "Golfo di Policasto" is from: *Regno di Napoli.* [1650?]

Map. https://brbl-dl.library.yale.edu/vufind/Record/4167377

Translations of Signs

Proprietà Privata, Private Property

Caccia di Cinghiali Consentita Solo a Gruppi con Permesso, Wild Boar Hunting Permitted Only for Licensed Groups

00, 00 (trail number)

Antico Passo dell'Osteria Bruciata, 17 – 8 – 86, Old Pass of the Burned Inn, 8 – 17 – 86

Divieto di Sosta: Lasciate Libero il Passaggio, No Stopping: Keep Area Clear

Bestiame allo Stato Brado, Open Range Livestock

Metandotto, Methane Pipeline

Vendesi, For Sale

Sodo dei Conti, Spring of the Counts

Purtroppo Qui Non Posso Entrare, Unfortunately I Cannot Enter Here

Transito Vietato agli Autoveicoli, Motorized Vehicles Prohibited

Festa de l'Unità, Unity Festival

Punto Panoramico, View Point

Fondo Chiso, Dead End

Impianto di Cattura: Divieto di Caccia, Animal Capture Area: No Hunting

Confine Del Parco: Rispetta La Natura, Park Boundary: Respect Nature

Sentiero 50, Trail 50

O passeggero che pasa per via non ti scordar di salutar Maria / Giovacchino Bonacci / Eresse l'anno 1902, O traveler who passes this way do not neglect to greet Mary / Giovacchino Bonacci / Erected in the year 1902

Attenti al Tubo, Mind the Pipe

Divieto di Scarico, Dumping Forbidden

Pericolo di Incendio, Fire Danger

Azienda Faunistico Venatoria Sintigliano: Caccia Consentita ai Soli Autorizzati, Stigliano Wildlife Hunting Reserve: Hunting by Permission Only

S. Antonio 1935, Saint Anthony 1935

Divieto di Pesca: Zona di Protezione, No Fishing: Protected Area

Frana !, Landslide Danger

Caduti Massi, Falling Rocks

Azienda Faunistico Venatoria, Wildlife Hunting Reserve

Monumento Isolato, Isolated Monument

Discarico in Sequestro Giudiziario, Dumping Grounds Seized by Court-Order

Casa Pericolante, Unstable House

Antichità, Antiquity

Percorso Pittoresco, Scenic Byway

Curiostià Naturale, Natural Curiosity

In Caso di Neve o Gelo, In Case of Snow or Ice

Vendesi Casa in Montagna, Mountain House for Sale

Punto Turistico, Touristic Point

Divieto di: Cacca Pesca Pascolo Transito, Forbidden: Hunting Fishing Livestock Transit

Divieto di: Accesso / Raccolta di Funghi Tartufi e Prodotti del Bosco, No Trespassing / No Gathering of Mushrooms Truffles or Forest Products

Dal Balcone di Questa Casa dal 1911, Viene Rappresentato il Volo dell'Angelo / Addi' 1 luglio 2001 / l'Amministrazione Communale, The Flight of the Angel has been Depicted on the Balcony of this House Since 1911 / On this Day of 1 July 2001 / The Municipal Administration

Allevamento Selvaggina, Game Breeding

Qui Non Si Fa Credito, No Credit Given Here

Strada Praticabile con Difficoltà, Rough Road

Vietato Fumare, No Smoking

Strada Sdrucciolevole, Slippery Road

Zona Militare: Invalicabile, Military Zone: Off Limits

Divieto Assoluto di Scarico, Dumping Strictly Forbidden

Rovine: Pericolo di Crollo, Ruins: Danger of Collapse

No Borse, No Bags

Divieto di Transito, No Thoroughfare

Rifugio Non Accessible, Shelter Closed

Vietato Attraversare i Binari, Crossing Tracks Forbidden

 , City Center

Footnote References

1. Da Vinci, Leonardo. "300. On the Colour of the Atmosphere." *The Notebooks of Leonardo da Vinci*. Translated by Jean Paul Richter. New York: Dover, (1888) 1970.

2. Ebrey, Patricia. "Taking Out the Grand Carriage: Imperial Spectacle and the Visual Culture of Northern Song Kaifeng." *Asia Major* 12, no. 1 (1999).

3. Braudel, Fernand. *The Mediterranean and the Mediterranean World in the Age of Philip II*. Vol. 1. Translated by Siân Reynolds. Berkeley: University of California Press, (1972) 1995.

4. Smailbegović, Ada. "7000 Things that Appear after the Yard Disappears. From *The Cloud Notebook*." *Pelt v.4: Feminist Temporalities*. Brooklyn: Organism for Poetic Research, 2017.

5. Lister, Diane, Mim A. Bower and Martin K. Jones. "Herbarium specimens expand the geographical and temporal range of germplasm data in phylogeographic studies." *Taxon* 59, no. 5 (2010).

6. Robertson, Lisa. "II [What is this tint that in the shrill cress.]" *XEclogue*. Vancouver: New Star Books, 2006.

7. Moser, Anna. "Two Landscapes." *Pelt v.4: Feminist Temporalities*. Brooklyn: Organism for Poetic Research, 2017.

8. Mead, William Edward. "Italy in English Poetry." *PMLA* 23, no. 3 (1908).

9. Rawlings, Angela. *Wider : B-side : rarities and remixes from Wide slumber for lepidopterists*. New York: Belladonna, 2006.

10. Shakespeare, William. *King John*. London: Printed by Tho. Cotes, for Iohn Smethwick, 1623.

11. Stanislawski, Dan. "Seeds for the Flowering of Tuscany." *Geographical Review* 67, no. 4 (October 1977).

12. Showerman, Grant. "Horace the Duality." *The Classical Journal* 6, no. 6 (March 1911).

13. Anderson, Karen Leona. *Punish Honey*. Durham: Carolina Wren Press, 2009.

14. Smethurst, David. "Mountain Geography." *Geographical Review* 90, no. 1 (January 2000).

15. *The Rig Veda*. Translated by Wendy Doniger. London: Penguin, 2005.

16. Toniolo, A. R. "Studies of Depopulation in the Mountains of Italy." *Geographical Review* 27, no. 3 (July 1937).

17. Walker, D. S. *A Geography of Italy*. New York: E. P. Dutton & Co, 1958.

18. Shelley, Percy. "Passage of the Apennines." *Posthumous Poems*. Edited by Mary Shelley. London: C. H. Reynell, 1824.

19. Niedecker, Lorine. *Collected Works*. Edited by Jenny Penberthy. Berkeley: University of California Press, 2002.

20. Boreen, Orinithalius. "The Relative Enchantments of Becoming Temporarily Bewildered." *Discrete* 44, no. 4 (2007).

21. Simpson, Natalie. "similar figures." *accrete or crumble*. Vancouver: LINEBooks, 2006.

22. Pezzi, Giovanna, Carlo Ferrari and Marcello Corazza. "The Altitudinal Limit of Beech Woods in the Northern Apennines (Italy). Its Spatial

Pattern and Some Thermal Inferences." *Folia Geobotanica* 43, no. 4 (2008).

23. Watson, Clare S. "The Vegetational History of the Northern Apennines, Italy: Information from Three New Sequences and a Review of Regional Vegetational Change." *Journal of Biogeography* 23, no. 6 (November 1996).

24. Roberts, Michael. "Rome Personified, Rome Epitomized: Representations of Rome in the Poetry of the Early Fifth Century." *The American Journal of Philology* 122, no. 4 (Winter 2001).

25. Tasso, Torquato. "Al Signor Gaspare Micinelli." *Penguin Book of Italian Verse.* Translated by George Kay. Harmondsworth: Penguin, 1958.

26. Dench, Emma. *From Barbarians to New Men: Greek, Roman, and Modern Perceptions of Peoples from the Central Apennines.* Oxford: Clarendon Press, 1995.

27. Alighieri, Dante. *La Divina Commedia.* Bari: Gius. Laterza & Figli, (1320) 1933.

28. Campana, Dino. "La Verna." *Orphic Songs.* Translated by Charles Wright. Oberlin: Oberlin College, (1913) 1984.

29. Watson, Clare S. "The Vegetational History of the Northern Apennines, Italy: Information from Three New Sequences and a Review of Regional Vegetational Change." *Journal of Biogeography* 23, no. 6 (November 1996).

30. De Quevedo, Francisco. *Selected Poetry of Francisco de Quevedo.* Translated by Christopher Johnson. Chicago: University of Chicago Press, 2009.

31. Jepson, Tim. *Wild Italy.* San Francisco: Sierra Club Books, 1994.

32. Walker, *A Geography of Italy.*

33. Celati, Gianni. *Verso la foce.* Milano: Feltrinelli, 1989.

34. Bertolini, Giovanni, Nicola Casagli, Leonardo Ermini, and Claudio Malaguti. "Radiocarbon Data on Lateglacial and Holocene Landslides in the Northern Apennines." *Congrès Natural Hazard Symposium of the European Geophysical Society's XXV General Assembly* 31, no. 3 (2004).

35. Watson, Clare S. "The Vegetational History of the Northern Apennines."

36. Pasolini, Pier Paolo. "L'Appennino." *Le ceneri di Gramsci.* Milano: Garzanti, 1957.

37. Piccinini, D., L. Margheriti, L. Chiaraluce, and M. Cocco. "Space and Time Variations of Crustal Anisotropy During the 1997 Umbria-Marche, Central Italy, Seismic Sequence." *Geophysical Journal International* 167, no. 3 (December 2006).

38. "Soci è." *Proloco Soci.* prolocosoci.it/il-paese

39. Kertzer, David. "Participation of Italian Communists in Catholic Rituals: A Case Study." *Journal for the Scientific Study of Religion* 14, no. 1 (March 1975).

40. Dawson, Edward. "What's in a Name: Apennines." *The History Files.* historyfiles.co.uk.

41. Sacchetti, Franco. *Penguin Book of Italian Verse.* Translated by George Kay. Harmondsworth: Penguin, 1958.

42. Coolidge, Clark. *The Crystal Text.* Los Angeles: Sun and Moon Press, 1995.

43. Mitchell, John. Review of Edmund G. Gardner, *Dante and the Mystics. The Modern Language Review* 8, no. 4 (October 1913).

44. Hofmann, Paul. "Taking to the Highway in Italy." *New York Times*, April 26, 1987.

45. Hawthorne, Nathanial. *The Marble Faun, or, The Romance of Monte Beni, Vol. I.* Boston: Houghton Mifflin, 1890.

46. Remein, Dan. "Dog song." *Picket Song. Dispatches from the Poetry Wars.* dispatchespoetrywars.com

47. Benesch, Otto. "Liss's 'Temptation of St Anthony'." *The Burlington Magazine* 93, no. 585 (December 1951).

48. Leader, Scott. *A Nook in the Apennines, or, A Summer Beneath the Chestnuts.* London: C. Kegan Paul, 1879.

49. Guerra, Tonino. *Abandoned Places.* Translated by Adria Bernardi. Toronto: Guernica, 1999.

50. McNeill, J. R. *The Mountains of the Mediterranean World.* Cambridge: Cambridge University Press, 1992.

51. Patton, Julie Ezelle. *Notes for Some (Nominally Awake).* New York: Portable Press, 2007.

52. Pezzetta, Amelio. *Casa rurale, ambiente, agricoltura e società a Lama dei Peligni dal 1700 ai giorni nostri.* Monfalcone: Tipografia Savorgnan, 1994.

53. Leopardi, Giacomo. "La sera del dì di festa." *Penguin Book of Italian Verse.* Translated by George Kay. Harmondsworth: Penguin, 1958.

54. Wiles, Bertha H. "An Exhibition of the Fountain." *Bulletin of the Fogg Art Museum* 4, no. 2 (March 1935).

55. Stanisci Angela, Maria Laura Carranza, Giovanni Pelino and Alessandro Chiarucci. "Assessing the Diversity Pattern of Cryophilous Plant Species in High Elevation Habitats." *Plant Ecology* 212, no. 4 (April 2011).

56. Poliziano, Angelo. "Baccanale." *Penguin Book of Italian Verse.* Translated by George Kay. Harmondsworth: Penguin, 1958.

57. Johnston, Charles. "Sonnet on the Apennines." *A Collection of Poems: Chiefly Manuscript, and from Living Authors.* Edited by Joana Baille. London: Longman, Hurst, Rees, Orme, and Brown, 1823.

58. Smith, Catherine Delano. "Ancient Landscapes of the Tavoliere, Apulia." *Transactions of the Institute of British Geographers* 41 (June 1967).

59. Wilson, Ernest H. *Aristocrats of the Trees.* New York: Dover, (1930) 1974.

60. Scappettone, Jennifer. "Delection Even." *Dame Quickly.* Brooklyn: Litmus, 2009.

61. Whitehouse, Ruth D. "The Megalithic Monuments of South-East Italy." *Man* (New Series) 2, no. 3 (September 1967).

62. Jackson, Thomas Graham. *A Holiday in Umbria.* London: John Murray, 1916.

63. Whitfield, J. H. Review of *Contemporary Italian Poetry*, by Carlo L. Golino. *The Modern Language Review* 58, no. 3 (July 1963).

64. Cambell, Thomas. "Life of the Poet." *The Sonnets, Triumphs and Other Poems of Petrarch.* Edited by Thomas Cambell. London: George Bell and Sons, 1879.

65. Niedecker, Lorine. *Collected Works.*

66. Oswald, Alice, "Dunt: a poem for a dried up river." *Falling Awake.* London: Penguin, 2016.

67. Mayer, Bernadette. "The Way to Keep Going in Antarctica." *A Bernadette Mayer Reader*. New York: New Directions, 1992.

68. Sebald, W. G. *The Rings of Saturn*. Translated by Michael Hulse. New York: New Directions, 1998.

69. Beckett, Samuel. *Cascando*. New York: Grove, 1963.

70. Skinner, Jonathan. "Windows." *Poetry at Sangram*. (November 2016). poetry.sangamhouse.org

71. Mayer, Bernadette. "Tsatsawassa." *Poetry State Forest*. New York: New Directions, 2008.

72. Mead, William Edward. "Italy in English Poetry." *PMLA* 23, no. 3 (1908).

73. Toniolo, A. R. "Studies of Depopulation."

74. Longfellow, Henry Wadsworth. "Divina Commedia." *The Poetical Works of Longfellow*. Edited by Horace Scudder. Boston: Houghton Mifflin, (1893) 1975.

75. Calvino, Italo. *On a winter's night a traveler*. Translated by William Weaver. London: Minerva, 1992.

76. Venturi, Robert, Denise Scott Brown, and Steven Izeneur. *Learning from Los Vegas.* Cambridge: MIT Press, 1972.

77. Johnson, Kent. "Into the Heat-Forged Air." *Chicago Review* 53/54, no. 4 (Summer 2008).

78. Massar, Phyllis D. "Presenting Stefano della Bella." *The Metropolitan Museum of Art Bulletin* 27, no. 3 (November 1968).

79. Ruskin, John. "The Stones of Venice." *The Complete Works of John Ruskin.* Vol. 10. Edited by E. T. Cook and Alexander Wedderburn. London: G. Allen, (1853) 1904.

80. Ariosto, Ludovico. *Orlando Furioso.* Edited by L. Caretti. Torino: Einaudi, (1516) 1966.

81. Pasolini, Pier Pasolini. "La scomparsa delle lucciole." *Scritti corsari.* Milan: Garzanti, 1975.

82. "Vastrogirardi Samnites: Vastogirardi Italic Temple." *Abruzzotoday.com* (this site has ceased to exist)

83. Barker, Graeme, John Lloyd and Derrick Webley. "A Classical Landscape in Molise." *Papers of the British School at Rome* 46 (1978).

84. Crawford, M. H., W. M. Broadhead, J. P. T. Clackson, F. Santangelo, S. Thompson, M. Watmough, E. Bissa, and G. Bodard. *Imagines Italiciae: A Corpus of Italic Inscriptions.* Bulletin of the Institute of Classical Studies Supplement 110, Volume II (2011).

85. Giscombe, C. S. *Giscome Road.* London: Dalkney Archive, 2005.

86. Ginsborg, Paul. *Italy and Its Discontents: Family, Civil Society, State 1980-2001.* London: Penguin, 2001.

87. Muldoon, Paul. "The More a Man Has the More a Man Wants." *Poems 1968-1998.* New York: Farrar Straus and Giroux, 2001.

88. Allen, Effie Alger. "Song of the Hearse." *Poetry* 32, no. 6 (September 1928).

89. Wordsworth, William. "Memorials of a Tour in Italy, 1837." *William Wordsworth: The Poems, Vol. 2.* New Haven: Yale University Press, 1977.

90. K., C. "Nature in Ovid" *The Classical Weekly* 16, no. 3 (October 16, 1922).

91. Day Lewis, Cecil. "A Time to Dance." *Collected Poems*. London: Hogarth Press, 1954.

92. Das, P. K. "The Earliest Expression of Delight in Mountains in the Poetry of the Eighteenth Century." *The Modern Language Review* 23, no. 2 (April 1928).

93. Ferraris, Roberta and Riccardo Carnovalini. "La Montagna minaciata." *Camminaitalia: Seimila chilometri dalla Sardegna alle Alpi*. Milano: Mondadori, 1995.

94. Van Buren, Albert. "The Geography of Ancient Italy. Part I." *The Classical Journal* 8, no. 7 (April 1913).

95. Spallanzani, Abbe Lazzaro. *Travels in the Two Sicilies and Some Parts of the Apennines*. Translated by Pinkerton, John. In *A General Collection of the Best and Most Interesting Voyages and Travels in all Parts of the World, Many of which are Now First Translated into English. Volume the Fifth*. London: Longman, Hurst, Rees, and Orme, Paternoster-Row; and Cadell and Davies, in the Strand, 1809.

96. Spallanzani, Abbe Lazzaro. *Travels in the Two Sicilies and Some Parts of the Apennines.*

97. MacDonell, Anne. *In the Abruzzi.* London: Chatto & Windus, 1908.

98. Wilson, Rachael M. "After-words." *Pelt v.1: Skin of Space.* Brooklyn: Organism for Poetic Research, 2012.

About the Author

Patrick Barron grew up in the Pacific Northwest, lived in Northern Ireland, the Netherlands, and Italy for a number of years, and is now based in Boston, where he teaches at the University of Massachusetts. He as been awarded grants and prizes from the NEH, the NEA, the Fulbright Program, and the Academy of American Poets. His poems, essays, and translations have appeared in publications such as *Ditch, Boneshaker, Basalt, Words Without Boundaries, Poetry East, The Argotist, Softblow, Interdisciplinary Literary Studies, Forum Italicum, Two Lines, Paideuma, Italica,* and *Modernism/modernity.* His books include *Terrain Vague: Interstices at the Edge of the Pale*; *Towards the River's Mouth,* by Gianni Celati; *Haiku for a Season, Haiku per una stagione,* by Andrea Zanzotto; *The Selected Poetry and Prose of Andrea Zanzotto*; and *Italian Environmental Literature: An Anthology.*

www.ingramcontent.com/pod-product-compliance
Lightning Source LLC
Chambersburg PA
CBHW030120100526
44591CB00009B/465